BONE WILLOWS

BONE WILLOWS

poems

James Engelhardt

Book design by Selena Trager

Library of Congress Cataloging-in-Publication Data
Names: Engelhardt, James, author.
Title: Bone willows / James Engelhardt.
Description: Pasadena, CA: Red Hen Press, [2018]
Identifiers: LCCN 2017033065 | ISBN 9781597099059 | eISBN 9781597099172
Classification: LCC PS3605.N447 A6 2018 | DDC 811/.6—dc23
LC record available at https://lccn.loc.gov/2017033065

The National Endowment for the Arts, the Los Angeles County Arts Commission, the Ahmanson Foundation, the Dwight Stuart Youth Fund, the Max Factor Family Foundation, the Pasadena Tournament of Roses Foundation, the Pasadena Arts & Culture Commission and the City of Pasadena Cultural Affairs Division, the City of Los Angeles Department of Cultural Affairs, the Audrey & Sydney Irmas Charitable Foundation, the Kinder Morgan Foundation, the Allergan Foundation, the Riordan Foundation, and the Amazon Literary Partnership partially support Red Hen Press.

First Edition
Published by Boreal Books
An imprint of Red Hen Press
www.borealbooks.org
www.redhen.org

ACKNOWLEDGMENTS

These poems have appeared previously in the following journals: *Blood Lotus*: "Working the Claim"; *Cirque*: "Boreal Halloween"; *Hawk & Handsaw*: "Uncontrollable Journey" (published as "Midwinter Journey"); *HeartWood Literary Magazine*: "Shadowboxing the Shaman"; *Ice Floe*: "Moving Up"; *Poecology*: "In the Sky, the Mountains"; *Route 7 Review*: "The After Party"; *Spoon River Poetry Review*: "Only Connect"; *Terrain.org*: "Wintering in the Place," "Boreal Valentine"; *The Fourth River*: "Framing the Day" (published as "Building the Frame"), "Before Aleph".

First, my deepest gratitude and love to my wife, Dana Kinzy. This book is for her. And Wendy, our fox princess.

Jeremy Schraffenberger, Emily Wall, and Jeremy Pataky read early drafts of the manuscript. This book is better for their attention and insights.

I offer my deep gratitude to Peggy Shumaker for her belief in my abilities over many years. I am especially grateful for her careful reading, precise feedback, and support of this collection.

I also want to thank Hilda Raz for her rigorous, unsentimental approach to thinking about words on a page. She is an extraordinary teacher, and any lapses in the book are mine alone.

There's also a debt I should mention to John Janovy, Jr., biologist and author, who gave me permission to put a lot of biology in poems. I thank him for that.

Any poetry collection is the work of many hands and holds within it the traces of myriad influences. This book is no exception. If I have met you on the path and we shared work, talked about poems, convinced each other to buy and read a particular collection, sent each other to journals or online postings, then you are here in these pages.

CONTENTS

III. ALL THIS LIGHT

IV. LIKE LICHEN

V. SOUND OF BREATH

VI. BRIMSTONE AND SOAPSTONE

BONE WILLOWS

BONE WILLOWS

We pause on the road, a cow moose and me,
and in a moment she vanishes like a magic trick.
I drive on home, to cut willows

from the roadside ditch and south bank—
scrubby ones that climb down our sledding hill.
With a few limb-saw strokes, the bones fall

as if a shaman's consultation telling me
to travel, meet the moon on the black spruce path,
whip willows into baskets and beehives.

Saw in hand, what truth do I find? A spine of hills,
a river. And those who came before me, envious,
require me to hold this present close

to root if I can. So I go on, and the willows
weave us together—that moose, those ancestors—
stitch sky to ground, and hold us up.

I

TAIGA PATHS

HIGHBUSH

We'll be very cranberry
along the bog bank, smelling
like dogs—
"I want one," our girl says.
Dog or berry? But the frost
hasn't sharpened the nubs to sweetness
and nobody wants winter
now that we have light.

"I didn't mean to," she says. "The dog
followed me here."
And who wouldn't give it to her?
But it's a sled dog,
and our couch has no runners
our heat steam-warm
when a husky
will want to sink under snow.

Don't we all say I want you
to have this? To make you happy?
The sun keeps shifting its brassy eye
mesmerizing trees, blueberries,
the fireweed wrapping the season
like a gift I can't give
though I try again and again
standing in this stream,
rocks rolling under my feet.

NO SNOW, YET

Birthday ribbons sink, pulled down
through air never too cold for snow,

for marriage, for children
to freeze to lampposts.

My friend, can you believe fields
empty of snakes and ticks?

The U-Hauls and semis that
sway like ships over the frost heave

cargo sometimes tipping, bursting
unribbed in Yukon Territory?

But the harder thing to know
is the useful emptiness

we don't notice,
like a basket that must be empty

or the shadow of an umbrella.
We hold the forests of our lungs

but breath always escapes,
like doors when they open

and close
on weather, a steady wearing.

One follows the other up
so the marriage tilts like a truck

from birthday to anniversary
and we wait

for winter
to bury

the dog shit in the yard.
Soon snow will come

not as a blanket, but a door
for sleds and pulks never imagined

and the aurora sparking like silk
over the shocked white quilt.

SONG OF FORGETTING

One day becomes the next and the next
and a month has passed and no letter
comes from your younger self.
The salmon hold no papers, the caribou

yield no alphabet,
but the sun's reincarnation
runs the brain
forward into its pine box.

What message
could you send
that would make
any sense to a child?

In the White Mountain foothills
sun circles overhead, almost sinks north,
before it's back again, and animals
wander, eyes blazing with light.

Loose skin might as well be fur,
any morning stiffness a fin,
the evening's usual martini
a body of quills.

Easter passed.
No eggs or chocolate,
and the sun
circles again without a note.

THICKET

willow stubble switches
out of white cones of drifted snow
and no snowshoe hare thinks violence
no child spared or spoiled
during deep coverage season

foxes denned up nearby
dream of blood chase, of grasshopper
crunch air, of honeyed feast midsummer

alder and birch hard and white
around steaming buildings,
lights vague behind ice-crusted windows

men have habits of mind
they control as well as the hare
that moves away from the dog's traces
the claw prints like a call
into an empty kitchen

CORNER SHOT

I missed you, he says,
rifle exhaling a pale twist

what can I give you,
she asks,
I have
these chess pieces
and a mandolin

I never miss, he says,
no price
for this old sled

I want to hold you, she says,
but you keep moving,
you keep looking away

like stepping into a canoe
not pulled up the bank

a missed strike
ax's one tooth
chewing air

the cats are here,
she says,
the last dog
clipped into the line

a comb, he says,
a yarn swift

THE A-FRAME IN THE TAIGA

in a steady stand of mirrors:
a man with razor soap beard,
his wife pulling her eyelid down

roots wrapping
birch next to aspen
limbs lapping trees hard to separate

not quite each other
tea at breakfast
or a soft drink with oats

a scrape of bird claw
chair across wood
as near as bread or eggs

THE AFTER-PARTY

The evening had been full of words.
Guests waited until the toddler had gone to bed
to gather with their cups near the one tall window.
They pointed to the waxing gibbous moon
low over the house to the south.
Glow over the short expressway, smudged
by clouds across black sky.

"Oh," they said, pointing, "let's turn out the light.
Let's see if the glow will turn our faces
that same yellow." And with the lamps dark
the words sighed off their shelves
until they stood empty as parchment
and the walls held up only moon and clouds,
the roof's bare line a street away.

SUNRISE

Then one February day the sun
sharpens the trail to the office door
and greets you on the turn home,
key in hand—spruce shadow stretches,
goddess reaching, pressing
insistent fingers to eyelids.

You'll miss that goddess in June and July,
but she'll be back to hold you
soon enough, forever. The thought flickers
with fencerow chickadees—
first time in months they've abandoned
the heat-halo around buildings and feeders.
Fog steams the path rising
to the road and you turn toward sun.

"NOW" SAYS THE CLOCK

tall grass
tips with last night's rain
light held on leaves and seed heads
makes me kneel
yes even at the wet edge
fireweed opening at the top
blossoms blown

left knee crunches
I'm silent now
neighbors asleep
the field
purple and crystal
and unbearable

around me
mountains roar against sky
against clouds drifting
across the faces of our tight houses

SETTLING DUST

I only know grasping—
my hold on handles, car keys
dropped outside safety,
forty below rounded
with a little snow.

The keys a quick frost,
the shock hot,
a burn on a warm palm.

Green aurora sinuous
as a slalom dragon offering
fortune, long sight.
"There is a path," she says,
and I try to learn to let go.

The keys jangle,
angles feathering the teeth
and millings.
Behind the door, a gift.

The door and its handle:

a lesson
the hoar of my heart
will not learn
though I stand
so close to emptiness.

PERMAFROST SUN ROT

a boreal cabin trapper shims
his way to balance
pours less tea, balance to cup lip
but then he wouldn't care

foundation voles shift their nest
to the best new angle, no context
beyond warmth, or protein,
or sharp-tipped shadows

sun warmer now each season
Winter's old-man hands a bit pinker
ear tips flaking now
ice drains out, hole slumps dirt shoulders
and he simply shims

AUBADE

bare aspens nod
their spring greeting
east, west,
a rare wind

sky unknits,
opens the barrel
staves of hills
rolling up to stars

breath again,
twig limbs write
the note I'll leave
on your stained pillow

II

TRYING THE NAMES

LEFT HAND, AND RIGHT

Lee stands above the Goldstream Valley
his new studio holding heat even
in the glittering early cold snap—
a lens of wood smoke caps the city

old gold ring rubs where you'd expect
his new partner back in the house
practicing silver notes from a gold flute,
arpeggios perhaps or simply scales

who knows these things, what musicians
might have in their chimed hearts—
what light a painter samples
from a new love's hair

they were wearing the rings
for months before anyone noticed
the birch-patterned bands,
silver—hammered and stamped

birches surround the house
filled with her dead husband's prints
a former drinking buddy
given to f-stops and swirling scotch

it's warm like that, the looking
over a frostbitten town, the trees
ice-crusted, but the hands are loose
on brush, keys, a strange heart

TAKING WHAT'S OFFERED

"How light is a wing?" someone asks
because the question sounds good
and should send us to books.

We're gathered around a fire to flirt
with each other's wives and husbands.
Our wine talk sends up thermals of breath

and we spiral beyond feathered edges, sound
thinning as we rise until we glide
alone without our tightening thoughts.

Moon shadows roll blue when we stagger out
into a night cold enough to freeze deep
into our bodies—sinuses, throats.

Car doors ease and creak.
We stagger into down-thick hugs,
the croak of closing and wheel crunch.

A wing, now, how light is that?
Raven fingers black and quick
against spiral stars.

BETWEEN BRIGIT AND OSTARA

The black bear hide stretched
to the plywood sheet's four corners

attracts no flies as it leans against
the visitor center wall.

A child skips past, yellow-haired doll
squashed tight to her body.

"Was that a bear?" She looks up at her mother
who says yes. "Oh!" Then more skipping,

under the arch of skulls and antlers and down
to the Chena River bank spotted

with slushy ice and the pyramids we build
so we can watch them tip during breakup.

The day is quiet, the river
rushes under its sheeting.

The season gathers its weight on its haunches
ready for bounding resurrection.

PARALLAX

The highway south follows the ridge
west, then away then west again
every drive west a drive away.

Hands hold the steering wheel's cross,
sun stalks the road, and I spin
along the roadbed, frost-heaved and dark

crossing under swans, eagles golden and bald
nesting in high-voltage stanchions
and above them croaking sandhill cranes.

Behind me, hilltops rounded like Appalachia,
sugar spoons for tea—more birch and willow—
but a comfort until the next turn.

Isn't this drive an escape? I can't tell
if the day is warm enough to open the window, to
let in what might come in, lost or hidden.

Climb to stark granite black, white, and glacial.
The sun hangs seven minutes longer today
like a marriage, changing, and the road turning away.

COLLAR AND LEASH

the tracks by the bike path
wolf-large between the pulk lines
through aspen, tamarack, birch

across the unlined street from us
a man keeps a boxer/bulldog mix
no ID collar, no harness

last week the dog kept pace
on my walk to the office,
too thin-skinned I thought

the dog surged ahead,
waited, stayed in step,
he peed a lot more

danced when he stopped,
nose to ptarmigan tracks—
a long channel of yellow snow

I have the collar and the leash,
our neighbor says one afternoon,
"where's the dog?"

the boxer I recognize doesn't want
his leash, doesn't miss his collar,
rises to the willowy landscape

WHAT YOU KNOW ABOUT THIS PLACE

It may be the guy in Carhartts,
pistol in a web holster on his hip,
on one knee inside the playground
at McDonald's, too cold to go outside,
and his daughter in pink spangles runs to him

but the gun isn't going to go off
not in this story, maybe not ever
outside of a range, or maybe a backyard—
empties lined up on cordwood

he can't go back to being the same man
not with this blood, these bones
his child warming her mittened hands
in the cab of his rusting truck

she'll hate him for something
and love him for something else.
Her box of a house filled to crushing
with toys and skin care products
that feel like the distance between
how a man loves a daughter
and how she loves him in return

the summer surges toward its end
and he'll tell this story of his last good days
years later to his daughter
who will leave the phone on speaker
while she rolls out cookies for her son
and behind her house the White Mountains

loop off the horizon while the sun spins overhead
and the moose over the ridge move
along, move along.

FREYA AND ODR

sun strikes the willow stand
bends shadows the shape of the wands
man and woman along on foot

the woman points at something
and the man might look as men do
distracted by his own mind, the sharp jaw

of some small idea and she laughs
maybe at his distance as he blinks
against the tall colors and tries to name

the names she knows for the walk they're taking
the distance of the willows from themselves
the weave of them and wave

the thicket grows after them, catkins
and snapped branches whole after the man
has pulled twigs for the woman's crown

I LOOK FOR A GATE IN THE BARRIER

Sun breaks above the foothills
cutting the outlines of trees
and I want to give this to you, my wife,
but it's been so long, silence reaching
beyond prism burst in the sinking field.

"Let's go," you had said, holding hands,
"into the wilderness of the future—
we'll be ambassadors to a satellite
full of pancakes and syrup
that has splashed down in a salty sea."
And you laughed strong,
throat jumping out.

There's a gift I'm keeping secret
like new ptarmigan tracks
white within the field of white, blank tracks
you can see but don't trust
so I keep them for myself,
their meaning hard to share.

When I get past the trees to the slough
the light is full yellow
and I wonder if love swells
like this sun rising again
each morning
offering nothing beyond nature.
And what do I have to give?
The hands I've mentioned, some weakness,
a knack for fire, and this poor shoulder
strapped to a small, orange burden.

BEFORE ALEPH

failure comes in trying to describe
the smell of relief at winter's end,
the Alaska plants springing back
from under snow, the stand of trees
and a balsam perfume I can't explain:
wood and laurel, musk and spicy rotting,
dry like wet cinnamon

maybe honey or amber comes near—
the kind of thing that draws insects
and the moose smell it, whatever it is,
the willows cracked, fractured,
white bones twisting

and I smell a bit of myself
puffing up from my jacket as I walk
and the smell comforts me more
than the smell of crisp, clean sheets in summer

the decay, the chemistry
of leaves coming around without thought or sound
all speaking about earth, about moon
the way an animal glows with no light

BEFORE COMPLETION

morning traffic leaves the complex
our neighbor skimming north
to his gold mine job

his wife tells him not to drink so much
take his cigarettes outside

he says to her: A whole pie, you ate
a whole pie at one sitting

everybody wants to ask someone else
what's wrong? what's wrong
with the weather? with you? with me?

the neighbor holds and nurtures a dream
of sucking and crushing gravel and she
dreams of pull tab after pull tab

over cans of thin beer they ask
why always cook that casserole?
why chase stars under water?

the sun will rise to the south tomorrow
our neighborhood fox jumps a ditch
trots through smoke

LOST, WANDERING

Deep tracks around the bike path
directionless, or all directions

like a choice you think you're making
to move your family—wife and son.

She might love you still, even
after the long nights brushing the baby's hair.

Cloven prints, like they say of the devil,
snow deep enough to catch

dewclaw depressions in new powder
dusting the short deck

built two summers ago,
the Halloween pumpkins frozen to it.

The tracks cross and cross each other.
It's cold together under the quilt

and who doesn't wonder about the blanket's stitches,
how they run together, wander,

like tracks down by the slough, almost
with a purpose, a plan that might go wrong.

But women always seem to back up,
adjust the thread, gather material,

move back down the path
they know, there.

WORK OF NOTT

January-crusted glitter
sharp on the shut eyelid

quiet sky, windless frost
crystal bulbs on trees

attention slow
and thick, unlit

Night opens gaps
as winter sinters

rustles black skirts
over town, river

chimes of light catch
against the pale blue

THE OTHER DARK

Heavy hooves split deep snow.
Moose tracks lead from browse
to browse, what's left
as the dark recedes and plants quicken.

The hoof tracks end roadside, as you knew
they must, brown fur stuck
to the teeth of ice the plows left.

A woman rides, smiles, hands folded
over her seatbelt, thinks there will be time
there is always time.

Lines converge, bowls fill
with spindrift, with blood, a valley
of silent animals keeping their counsel
about the weights of night.

Store-shelf moose grin stupidly, kayak snout
paddle antlers, ridiculous chopstick legs—
but tonight, a collision:

everyone walks away but the animal.
Phone calls to people who don't know,
who respond with "go back" when she says
the baby's OK, the ultrasound is OK.

Blue lights, red lights strobe shadows
as the guys from the mission squat, cut,
fill the buckets, gather, and reconfigure.

More tracks later. Daylight and hunger
balance against the bowl, the shock,
the possible other tracks, deeper bruises,
the traffic moving through.

III

ALL THIS LIGHT

WATER AND SMOKE

A new place, the same family
you've had for years. Words
roll between you like rocks
or, on a good day, trot like lynx

into a world you've never walked,
a soft place above the skull, perfume
useless as back closet silks
in this place of wool and bone.

You've lost words for the quiet glow
of a mountain just past dawn,
a wing unfolding in your chest
like a down vest opening and then

a different light, a different light
even at midnight, even in cloud.

BOREAL HALLOWEEN

Cold webs the quarter-year, Celts
and Saxons and Norse consult the dead
before the long night relaxes into starlight chips.

Town kids cluster at schools and churches,
costumes invisible as spirits under snow pants and parkas,
the sweet quarter candy harvest and laughter moon.

Smoothed metal cups and bowls, wooden tafl pawns,
a bent man runs calluses over thoughts
about what the shaman and witch told him

over a strong mushroom drink. A solace
a practice refined during nights like these, and longer.
Hands slip, thinking shifts to vapor.

The fence between worlds breaks
and a wolf's steam-cloud howl calls for a round
as young village men wait for the bush plane
with hot-blooded eagerness, their women alone.

TUNDRA CAROL

I sing the silence of nightfall snow
a song of November aurora

the song of sloughs hard enough
to park a fueled plane on

of sharp snow resting edge to edge
the night a solstice minute shorter

the book open above the path
the hushed flight set to music

THE NATURE OF THE THING

In my dream, I am a wolf
nipping at a fog running uphill,
flowing uphill, I cannot say
my throat is wrong, my tongue lolls
uncontrollable in the snowfield.

By fog I mean someone else,
some person, of course, or the idea
of a person, running away from the wolf,
and isn't a person like a fog?
Nothing but vapor, a shifting here

of thought, perhaps even intention,
something we might call love
on an evening rolling into night,
the mists rising from the river valley.
And I am running into the clouds,

a wolf trying to pull at the edge
of her, some lover I had,
or were we married some time past?
The mist rose-tinged and streaming
downhill like fear or ego,

and I'm beside her now, forcing
my teeth into the soft edge
as we plunge into taiga, aspen,
and then out into fields, travel,
maybe a child, a house, a car.

In the dream, I believe
we're part of a legend, a myth
sometimes dipping into some story, mist.
We both want something stable, even to love,
but I'm running and I can't stop.

PATTERNS OF LAND AND DRIFT

a snow wave slides
down banks pulling
willows into cervical curves

longer sun
reveals hidden skins—
today the first birds

magpies and flickers slip
through the almost-budding trees
crowding oily mud

bears will join us soon, scratching
at the new shoots that break
the surface of the exquisite earth

IF ONLY NIGHT

"I have something to tell you,"
the blonde insomniac whispers
in the clattering twilight

no ribboned song or gold-bright wings
the swallows are gone with the heat
and sandhill cranes labor for balance

who can stay when it's summertime hot?
who can stay when it's arctic and solid?
a dance step, a dance step, a sudden lift

when sundown finally slants her blade at us
all the windshields at the intersection
glitter with scars—cracked glass hearts

the babysitter brings half a salmon
and a vacuum pack of Dall sheep steaks
"I can't stay," she says, "with all this light"

TRANSUBSTANTIATION

"Garden needs to turn, tilled,"
she says to him
summer circling past bloom.
"Oh," he says.

Berries brighten corner-patch canes,
stitch cranberry wetdog to teabush spice,
days left until sundown,
taiga creaks, heaves.

"Our garden," she starts again
conversation like a dog on a line.
"The tiller," he says, "rusted."

Light in early summer
bites like a lemon
behind the eyes, a flare
of magnesium starlight
starching stardust brains.

"I won't," he says, fingers still, knotted,
and she's a half-round of lace.
"But wings are in the garden," she says,
"it needs lift."

BOOK OF REVELATIONS

A wife finds her husband's passwords
reaches like a fox after a vole,
delicate wedge sorting, making sense.

Summer's bright reveal opens sky,
one day lasts until
death, frost, bundling snow.

Passwords open tunnels, names
and numbers, answers more useful
than sun, than the water cycle
she was teaching their son after dinner.

She holds in her mind the network,
the dependency of atmosphere on a distant star,
the run of an animal into a den,

the routes all angled up, safe from flood.
If she keeps holding on,
she can wait for evening.

AUFEIS

New friends push up from the table
leaving the last of the mountain goat sausage
and pasta on our Fiesta plates.

We tell the stories of lives we've constructed,
storylines as comfortable as a bowl of hot grains
and a mug of coffee with a spoon of sugar.

"The breakup came around breakup, years ago,"
one of them said, the biologist or the chemist,
but the language was new

or maybe the hour was old, the bottles of wine
deeper than I remember, enough to hide
a narwhal, that arctic unicorn, or the thin surprise

of an aurora whipping as silent as fate,
as brilliant as an angel over the blooms
of snow gentled onto the dormant twigs.

"Breakup is coming," the other one says,
and I can't look at my wife, or his,
as the crescent moon rises like a serpent.

LUPERCALIA

Across the slough's ice
our neighbors' snow machines howl
a madness of glitter crystals spuming up.

For the festival night, we're frozen
nobody running naked through town
wolves jog nearby, silent.

Love songs scratch
in back bedrooms, ice-lined windows
the wavering boundaries

light and sound dizzy skin
comforters and sheets
shoved, gathered, and later smoothed

into a cornice of wool and polar fleece.
Breath settles into a slow pulse
and rides in hot silence

or in the blood
of the thousand small feet quiet on the snow,
secret hearts like embers.

Corner woodstove fires
bleed heat, that ancient welcome.
Open the door to the sun, and again sun.

MOVING UP

Keep driving. You can't get lost.
The Alaska Highway lurches tired
across taiga, tundra,
tumbles over basins and muskegs,
the shock and shock of bony mountains.

On a white gravel pull-out,
a young man looks at his map,
unwrinkled, graded flat with his hand,
the roadless stretches catching sun—
How old before you can't carry
all your rooms in a cash-on-the-barrel Toyota?

Do you think a girl waits for him?
Maybe.
And she might pick a banjo
while a waxing moon skirts aspens.
She whispers a chorus.
The moon will be dark beneath the cabin
before he arrives.

Imagine the explosion,
dining room sunburst
star-bright against the dinnerware,
his mother, his father . . .
What sharp tendrils scroll out.
How the elements all push
against each other, against the walls.

So he goes. Hands shoving
doors, his momentary wave propelling

the car, his burning books and cassettes,
over the plains north. North and west.
Mountains sprocket the window.
He puts the map away. He can hear
her singing on the shallow porch.

PREPARING TO ENDURE

she was tugging lines tight
cinched a fox-sized pelt
to the top of one of her two red sleds

just the ravens and I watched
as the semis of the freight company
pulled around the small snow patch
at the front office

a pink neck warmer up
around her ears, rising over her head
like a soft chimney

Peterbilts and Kenworths
grumbled and belched as they backed
to the bays and trailers—
rhythm of heavy, metal couplings

two sleds, a backpack, some cut-open
cases of dry food in her pick-up
as the sun came up, roadbed fogging

the ravens tarry on their way
beating from Wickersham Knob to here
to Ester Dome a local rhythm
unstringing roads, trackless path pulled up behind

IV

LIKE LICHEN

CONTRA DANCE

“ice will catch again”
a man says to a friend over the bed of a truck
a cloud of insects gathering

ten miles away the women
watch dogs in the yard
as they nip, jump, roll

sweet teeth snapping
on air and the women talk about the men
how they struggle to unknit their foreheads

water sinks, seeps into rivers
pushes ice up, shoves it along channels,
open for a long afternoon float

“oh it will break again,” they say, “miles apart
the push will come and it will all break again”

ONLY CONNECT

She wants to feed the moose, she tells me,
this little girl birthed in a Nebraska snowstorm.

We're born with large hearts,
as large as punch balloons

with tethers, but it's still hard to understand
why this heart keeps bounding away and snapping back.

The moose don't know, barely ankle deep
in the neighborhood snow.

In spring they will shed fur, a gift
as unintended as a parasite or virus

for the ptarmigan, chickadees, redpolls
that are not generous in turn

to beetles, flies, the larvae
our daughter reads about, reports back to us,

and steps into her polka dot boots
to stomp down the hill to hunt

in the weird light of summer
when the taiga fills its closets, mends coats.

And death rises like another step along a ridge,
a gift from a child.

FASTER, SPIN THE WHEEL FASTER

Stability seduces.
A child holds a stone in each hand:
this one is a toad, she says

one grandfather already dead.
Arctic spring bicycles down a bookcase,
ice and snow shock to flowers in forty-eight hours.

One morning in your early forties
you wake up with a cold and think
this could be the pneumonia that killed my father.

Summer's peak
hovers for three days like a full moon
and sags back toward jackets, sweaters,

wife and daughter clicking needles—
wool yarn organized into hats, scarves
and your wife pauses to shake her hand out.

Pull the blanket around your shoulders
as age drives pins into joints
and fingers curl into soft crabs.

A quick aside to a friend over a fire
and it's winter again, rolling dice indoors,
baking bread just to warm the house.

And then spring's purple light, budding aspen,
but it's too late, leaves open, summer.

AUGUST MORNING

Slough sliced by beaver half a dam away
from the big-bus morning rush of tourists
heading for the Parks Highway down
to the arching march of Alaska Range granite.

What moves, or would want to, on this old dog day?
Kayaks dew-damp and curved like lips
float gently in traffic's eddy. Play
needs to be done as much as work.

No fog, a clear look into birch and aspen
along the water. And then a roll of pelt
and the slow worker flips down to roots
below the paw prints gouging the bank.

Dark still beyond the bounds of office hours
but closing in daily on the trip to the park,
the bedtime stories, winter only a hint in wisping breath,
home a secret held against hard dark.

IN THAT GREAT LAND, THERE IS NO FIRE SUPPRESSION

nobody cares if lightning pops
and shatters spruce,
slouched black shoulders catch
sparks racing crown to crown

like an envelope on a coffee table
waiting for a husband to return,
the children off at a neighbor's house,
distant as Sunday,

shock, the rumble and rush
of flame across tundra, through taiga,
bounding up slopes
breaking into the long light

she sips a white tea, the leaves like lichen
leaching something like flavor
if she could taste anything, her nail polish
half removed, still sparkling like berries

it all grows back, not the same as it was—
looks a little less direct, conversation
directed at the dog, requests filtered
through children, a trusted brother

but the trees grow back, the moss
never gone for long, rhizomes matted
like a heat shield, a fiber blanket
as if the ice lens projected the world

NORTH IS ONLY NORTH

On the Alaska Highway,
sandhill cranes cutting the sky,
a retired electrician steers his RV,
his hand crooked and stained.

His future unspools as he looks
for something he can't find in his den,
at the IGA, waiting while his wife
knits evening to evening in front of the TV.

A porcupine staggers out and he slows,
slews across heaves, lines, a rainbow.
This mid-American life
feels easy to dismiss

if not for the terror gripping the wheel
their hearts jealous as you walk back
to your friends with a pitcher of beer
a handful of balloons for the kids.

THE PREPONDERANCE OF THE SMALL

She says she's too tired to walk.
We're climbing the grassy hill of fill dirt
between the condos, stepping carefully
over a shattered beer bottle, crushed
candy and empty wrappers, a dry turd,
a wrinkled condom. We are near the top,
where the path runs east-west, and we
started up from the south.

The sky behind the fire station crowds
with storm clouds, but we don't notice,
continue hiking up the dry grass.
We comment on the new shoots
and she slips, reaches out, and asks
to hold my hand. "Whoa," she says,
and we pause to admire big sticks,
rocks rounder than ice cream scoops,
the newly arrived moths.

A woman with a shepherd and poodle
takes the pair of them into the wild spit
below us, and we watch them squat.
My daughter fascinated by bowels, and I
notice the woman keeps walking.
On our last time downhill, she spreads her arms
croaks like a raven as I warn her—as I must—
to step carefully, to pay attention.
She asks to be carried as we turn toward home
and already she's larger in my arms.

BOREAL VALENTINE

Dana bends too far over the coffee table,
back cantilevered painfully as she colors
the lovebirds for Wendy's preschool cards,
and the girl herself carefully places
one butterfly sticker on top of another

precisely off-balance, like the snow outside.
It's so cold now that disrobing is work.

I remember budding trees, crocuses,
the glossy green nubs of daffodil beds
among the hay-drab yards of neighbors
and the smell of something like rot,
something like life seeping coolly down
from the mountain forests and into school.

But I'm developing a love of white and black,
of snow and spruce cutting sky—stars or dawn,
the streaming lights, or blue day opening
a wider eye as we each grow older, as Wendy
learns to lean in like her mother and write
the spindles and shoots of her name.

A AND NOT-A

the story starts with a man screen-hunched
reading a note from his beloved

it's an invitation to choose, two buttons to click,
one button will allow for great joy, the text reads,

the other offers something else, possibly apologies
but the sun has shifted in the time it takes to read

the glare erases his choices
the buttons will reappear, of course, but now

one of them reaches for a glass of wine
the sun catches the loose tea in the other's mug

which choice is which? one has a college logo
the other a rabbit

these two people huddled in their frame house
anticipate the coming season, have been shopping

this shirt looks good on you, those pants are slimming
and now they are home, years speeding through the house

leaving hair in the drains, fewer bottles of hard liquor,
less salt in the cupboards, his screen

still displays the choice and surely one of them
will reach out, a click, and that will be that

the fire will cool, and you know
choice cups the sunblown afternoon

WINTERING IN THE PLACE

She wakes to a day that seems colder,
her hip stiff, the sun shifted some small degree
rising a little north, gaining a little more height
like a pail handle held at this angle, now that.

A cup of tea, a short morning,
a walk around the neighborhood
for health, yes, so when her daughter calls
she'll hear the shock of the day's chill
across the ether to someplace cornstalked.

She knows the ravens don't wait for her,
croak and woodblock their calls for something else
not her. They do not wait for her
and her fur anorak, she brings along
no food for birds, no food from her.

A heavy spatter of snow splashing
as a ptarmigan pulls hard into the air,
like a pear tossed from one hand settling quickly
into the next, a safe bank a few yards away.

Woman and bird square off the block, five
left turns, then six, black tail tips,
mukluk shuffle, mittens on doorknob
and why not think of chicken, a nice roast,
a phone call, quick sundown and long starlight.

BERNHARD AND ELISE

the man holding trekking poles
touches each steep edge of the path
"they never meet," he says
into the billow of mosquitoes

"we share a net," says the woman
cinching her daypack tight to her back,
"I gathered the weave loosely
and cut to fit our hats"

you can walk from here up to the sky
but not reach it, clouds retreat
into fog, into gaps in fog, into air
reaching for the memory of a smell

"this side we'll call mountain goat,"
he says, tapping, and she answers, "this side
we'll call pintail duck"
and they set themselves onto the path

leaving illegible footsteps—
scat means something, fireweed
means something when cottoned out,
there will be stars when I can't reach you

NEW HOUSE

Fledglings hit the window,
second round of loose feathers this summer.

The rain comes down again
so we're learning about light as we watch

the sun shift shadows all week—
dinner and its candle clatter and shimmer

with a different glare each day or two.
The silence stays steady

except for the sometime thump of a small body
mistaking clarity for space you can pass through.

V

SOUND OF BREATH

FRAMING THE DAY

We are corrected at breakfast:
the owl's sound is "who," our daughter says,
and hoots for us delighting in memory
and the stretch of day before her, friends
who will arrive at preschool.

But this was a baby owl, we say,
and as large already as two housecats
held side-by-side at the shoulder.
It shrieked a short "eee" as sharp
as its new beak as it keened
for its family close by but quiet.

We remembered together the loose feathers,
another of the summer's fledglings,
and how it rose like a clouded moon
into the white spruce
as we stood surrounded by owl calls,
sunset hiding details at midnight.

Our daughter nods, knowing her own
night calls and solitary fears,
and tells a story of tigers and owls,
of fantastical leaps and near misses,
that ends with a crash
into a window and a feathery death.

Breakfast berries and oatmeal
swallow the dark moment. Her spoon clatters.
"What will my friends be wearing?"
she asks of us, eyes wide,
"Maybe owl costumes."

FLIGHT

We agree not to resist
let the sled
take us downhill
a rush like children
meeting a parent in an airport.

The static, the crystal spray
around you
behind you that sound—
who's screaming?
a bounce and bound

hold tight
something must give:
the direction, the drive,
the sled, or you.

The high of joy flying
downhill

spinning to a stop
a brief check,
spindrift settling.
Take off
again, uphill,
white laughter.

A SLIP OF SUN

We spend the morning dyeing eggs.
The flimsy wire dipper, the weak
chipboard drying rack. I recall the muddle
of adults trying to tie crosses
to paper-white eggs in a miasma of vinegar.

Slick puddles before ground thaws to mud.
Freshets wink at geese and cranes,
and they splash and stab landings
where foxtail and willow will rise again
furious in the long green days.

Ptarmigan in winter white and sable
flutter and peck around forest-edge willows.
Air clings to winter. Climate cuts. We tuck eggs
in frozen pockets and twig-dark trees.

RIVER'S HEAD

I haven't meant to collect these stories—
the contractions, dilations, the deep softenings.

How many of my high school classmates
graduated with their own babies in the audience?

The cards in the stationery aisle say
that the child is born from the love

two people have for each other.
But liquor is quicker.

Pitocin, epidural, monitors strapped on,
drips started while the ice storm moves through.

Labor and the history of labor
the old gurney-to-anesthetic-and-here's-your-baby.

I never listened to my own story,
the body from body more than unnerving.

In Piedmont North Carolina I listened
to my friend Mickey Jo on her son's birthday.

We're close to Ostara again, and I tell my daughter
on her fourth year that spring is behind the bunnies,

the eggs, the resurrection of the bears and salmon
as we don't splash the ice puddles lining the road.

Her namesake writes to say
she'll have another surgery after the last baby.

South of here, the world flutters in pastel
so lovely against the dull storm skies.

SPRING BRINGS ONLY EARLY DAWN

the beaver blinks awake,
slips out from his dam

snowmelt puddles still sharp with ice,
claw marks gouge the bank's mud

other scratches, too,
of a child fighting bed, a man

sliding his anger at his wife, a woman
pushing a knife through despair

the ravens always here but now ducks, too,
a few geese drop down

to lichens, arid swamplands, fantastical winters
when temper settles like snow

THE FAMILIAR CONDITIONS CHANGE BRINGS

change riots through the yard
summer solstice just past

after a month in the new house
daisies where two days ago
only lupine nodded, another crop
of sparrows and juncos hop,
spike up, and flush away to the spruce

fireweed blooms out the lowest purple rung
weather sways between warm and chill

we remain on our trajectories
cycling through hatch and bud
each half of the bed
as separate in the new light
as our cats from the birdfeeders

DAY REACHES POLE TO POLE

the dawn we summer through
burns birds into the sky
in sharp, brown lines
vining together the night haze
and stark-slant day

and when our bed is finally
pooled with blankets
we will look at each other
and at that moment

what will we know? how will we
tell our stories of devil's club, glaciers,
pony rides for our little girl?
the light clicks off
our eyes slick like river stones

IN THE SKY, THE MOUNTAINS

First fall colors in Alaska,
no plane trees, sweetgum, oak, maple,
our expected notes and tones of autumn.

On the hill heading up to Murphy Dome
shadows stutter across my face.
Dana clicks knitting, and Wendy
slides rubbery clothes on and off
her thumb-sized dolls.

A dip, a saddle between summits,
and the dome. Against the sky, a rock circle,
a fire pit, an air force globe to the east.

We could be giants, our bones standing on bones
down to the valley floor where frost
is a week behind. But instead we stagger
over ground rutted by ATVs, littered
with shotgun shells and empty cans.

We climb onto a white, standing rock
so we can see the river,
the mountain ranges north, south, west.
For our first time, Denali clears her head,
a distant, ghost goddess on the horizon.

Late night and the clouds scatter off
giving us our first sighting of the aurora,
weak as it twists over city light.
Did we hold each other while we watched?
I can't recall.

CHINOOK

A few gentle snows, enough weight
to bend a spider web. Yesterday
an odd wind slipped into town

like a curious bear rolling in
to check the songs a string band cinches
under bare bulbs in the sounding boards
of a plywood-and-chipboard living room.

A woman nods tap-and-stomp rhythm,
chill pings glass, frame flexes
a boyfriend in the next room forgets

to feed birch to the fire. Still,
the smoke trails off, the bear
shuffles a half-remembered dance,
the skeleton snow rattles down.

ORIENTEERING

it's too hot inside
volcanoes pucker linoleum
fires creep from wrapping paper

to wine bottle—
beyond the door
the small evening sun

almost January
cold as real as the north star
past the mothless streetlight

in houses, hands roll dough onto boards
houses packed with sugar
glow of want, of surfeit

an outline of stars scoops bent light,
but eventually, pastels will smear
the southern sky—light without heat

no sound but breath in the coat's hood
a square's turn to home
the moment raven-skirted

VI

BRIMSTONE AND SOAPSTONE

WORKING THE CLAIM

The cashier at Fred's tells the woman
at the card machine that her hair's almost back
but the boyfriend still isn't.
The pack of buns goes over the scanner
then the bag of chips.
"You should come to the party"
the food woman says. "It'll be fun
and Jackie will be so happy to see you again."

Spring flowers crowd the aisles near the door
and someone has set a lily in a RockStar can
next to the register. The flower
stirs a bit as the receipts and coupons ratchet out.

The cashier hands over the long looped ribbons.
"I might do that," she says,
and you can almost see the pick scars,
the places where blood was mined
for information and replaced
with a burn that traveled to her eyes
and is just now starting to settle out
like gold flakes in a pan.

"It's spring," she says as she pulls the bar off
slides it along the track above the belt.
"It's spring and I'm still here, ain't I?"

INTO LANGUAGE

Our little girl swoops her green fairy over
the bark-sided dollhouse her grandma sent

and in sunset light the wings flutter just a bit
so the girl's fingers close around air . . .

It's magic—a dream enjoying a deep hit
off its own logic, which suits the girl and fairy.

They search the rift we know
hasn't healed and splits each room, keeps

the center of the bed clear of birds
or creatures that creep under mossy blankets

to find another pair of paws or ears
but find only stone, a split, a silence.

The fairy flits between bookshelves,
knitting needles, cups, and cupboards.

The girl claps her hands, the moon is almost up,
a star darts, our eyes fill, we spread our arms wide.

STRENGTH OF THE SIGNAL

just a few years ago I wouldn't have known
what to call the strange dress
the older woman late to the lecture
was wearing as she moved to an aisle seat

this year, a thrill to see the garment
in Chicago and I wonder where she's
from in Alaska: my small city? a village?
now we're in this large room, tube lights

washing out color, the both of us
listening to a tall man reading a story
as he leans heavily on the podium

and though I've not lived long in Alaska
I feel better seeing this elder in her qaspeq
thinking about finger-stopping cold,
black-skirted ravens, new names for the world

UTOPIA, "A" TERMINAL

these gates just let you in
          no security

leaving the baby behind anchors anxiety
like a power-tool case muddy from the oil field
holding a seat for a young man gone
for coffee or morning beer

mothers yell in Athabaskan, Iñupiat
Xtratuf boots and ragged Carhartts—
nothing light here, no irony

bouncing baby,
          steaming coffee

he hands the kid back as she erupts
but he has to go, right?
He'll be back, he promises, but the wails
trail him. A few faces look up, smile.

We're all down here together, rifle cases stacked
weapons unloaded, prepared.
His path lifts into clouds
wisps cut with rattling props.

LINE OF SIGHT

Fog and rain cotton hillside erosion,
sink slick into the gaps and saddles
the highway rides through to get to town.

"Miserable day," one of them says.
"I was about to say 'beautiful,'"
says the other, leaning on the window.

Light pulls away from summer,
the monotonous sky a bellwether
of the descent into long dark.

"It's a song I can sing to," one says.
The other's hand stops halfway
to radio buttons, retreats to lap.

The berries are rioting
even as their leaves burn to red,
and, somewhere nearby, bears feast.

Up in the mountain pass the valley view,
but the bag on the floor opens,
papers spill across the storyline.

Brake lights blur before wipers clear them.
The argument they don't have is about work.

EDEN

daily earthquakes
groundshift thunder
young geology
kicking up peaks
crystal-thin mantle shifts
magma push back

when was it
earth stayed in place
broad-backed, wide-hipped
bucking horse
wild for you, for the next boy
a welcome place
the plants
the fur and who wears it
and feather, scales, and skin
slinking and sinking

fire and brimstone
fir and soapstone
roll of tide,
the troll a name
to reach down and give
to buck-toothed children
flushing in Holocene spring
glacial thrill giving in

a solar flare tears
away, apart, and back
invisible wave

sparking when it hits
magnetic field
a wavering, silent dervish

TABLETOP MOUNTAIN

in the saddle between
twin summits just wind
a shallow divide
where rock-field yields to plants

down the south face a boulder
catches the glazed sun
of summer late enough that a marten
lazing on the rock
is mottled brown and white

BEFORE THE ROUNDING

the blankets part cold,
turned down for both of you—
winter's blocky limbs tucked alongside
the orange cat and beagle-mix dog

windless night starless
and it's well after dark now,
switches clicking through the house

the kid's asleep
after the usual padding requests but now
just the white noise of even breathing

snow's falling again easing
margins and contrast, and outside
the fox who left prints at grass knots
has curled up in some musky den

snap off the bedside light,
you can hear your wife
shuffling on tiles—
the sink runs the clunk of pipes stops

a sudden dark appears in the hall
low groan as the bed shifts
another breath, a catch, another breath
and the night opens into emptiness
a snow-covered den, the cold of the bed

AT LESSONS

The city barely shakes the ice fog

starts rumors of a chinook. What will the spruce do

as the pallbearers stagger down the snow-packed steps

before men in gray beards and duct-taped coveralls?

How will cells survive the sudden warmth?

The foxes shake themselves—delirium of a green dream,

a ptarmigan wing—not a single body

in our valley will think spring.

UNCONTROLLABLE JOURNEY

the one road heading north
dead-ends in Deadhorse

the end is nigh and night spills
into the next day, there should be an end

Santa Claus stops at Deadhorse
leaves eleven months later, full of schnapps

you tell me your mother walked out,
headed north

you say you were too young
to pay attention, to notice

your father had taken
to drinking out of an old Christmas glass

three wise men, a baby,
and a star

you add these
to the list of places you can't go back to

LIGHT REMAINS

A friend stops by to tell me
about her dying husband, the process slow
like working deeper into a forest
no blizzard, not a blank white swallowing.

Like I notice dials set louder now
in the car, on my iPod, the hip
that feels stiff when I stand after the cushion,
the clocks I've let slow down and stop.

We walk backward into the snow,
she says, he can still tell some old stories,
but those have faded as he curls over
like local birches after the Thanksgiving storm

that came as surprise one mild autumn
and pulled the necks of the trees to the ground
the way a wrestler
tries to muscle each test case down

before the match ends
in sweat and exhaustion on rubber foam,
sun through an upper window
making the air stuffy and close.

He doesn't want to be a burden,
not as strong as he was,
and we're silent for a time
both of us understanding what we hold.

She puts down her teacup, a tremor
just before the base rests, and she adds
something about time, my time, but my watch
is broken and already the sun has set.

SHADOWBOXING THE SHAMAN

The raven appears, conjured
out of coal and spirited to the snowfield.
She's almost invisible, the sun behind her,
and she extends a wing, asks

if you're still paying attention,
mentions the squirrels knocking snow
out of the spruce, and can you see
those willow buds swelling?

This must be a dream, the white so deep
it's almost black, and the riverside air so warm.
Her other wing waves, a half-flap,
behavior that makes sense but accomplishes

nothing. "How did you get here?" she asks,
eyes like a chip of tiger beetle carapace,

Where did you come from, to be standing
hip-deep in an edgeless, opal field?
She prods you on what feels like your shoulder,
so you turn, turn, and keep going around

for a while: trees, then not, then mountains
cut by a river, and she asks, "Where are you going?"
just as you come back around, again,
coal clucking at you and the wheel of your feet.

BIOGRAPHICAL NOTE

James Engelhardt lived for five years in Fairbanks, Alaska, with his wife and daughter. He was active in the poetry community there. His poetry has appeared in *Ice Floe, Natural Bridge, North American Review, Terrain.org,* and many other journals. His critical work has appeared in the *Journal of the Midwest Modern Language Association* and *Mid-America Review.* He is an acquisitions editor at the University of Illinois Press.